WHERE DO YOU GET YOUR IDEAS?

Helping Young Writers Begin

by
Sandy Asher

illustrated by
Susan Hellard

Walker and Company
New York

First published in the United States of America
in 1987 by the Walker Publishing Company, Inc.

Published simultaneously in Canada by John Wiley & Sons
Canada, Limited, Rexdale, Ontario.

Library of Congress Cataloging-in-Publication Data

Asher, Sandy.
  Where do you get your ideas?

  Includes index.
  Summary: Describes how to find ideas for writing stories,
poems, and plays. Includes tips from well-known authors.
  1. Authorship—Juvenile literature. [1. Authorship]
I. Hellard, Susan, ill. II. Title.
PN147.A7227   1987   808′.02   86-28258
ISBN 0-8027-6690—0
ISBN 0-8027-6691-9 (lib. bdg.)

Printed in the United States of America

10 9 8 7 6 5 4 3 2 1

Book design by Laurie McBarnette

*For the teachers in my life
and the young writers and readers
I've met along the way*

*And with thanks to Claire Smith and the authors who
so generously contributed their special stories behind
the stories.*

Novels by Sandy Asher

Missing Pieces
Everything Is Not Enough
Things Are Seldom What They Seem
Just Like Jenny
Daughters of the Law
Summer Smith Begins
Teddy Teabury's Fabulous Fact

CONTENTS

1. **WHERE DO IDEAS COME FROM?**   1

2. **HOW MANY WAYS CAN THIS BE DONE?**   4
   Waking Up to Poetry

3. **STORIES BEHIND THE STORIES**   11
   Lloyd Alexander, Lois Lowry, Jan Greenberg, and Carol Kendall

4. **HOW MANY WAYS CAN ANYTHING BE DONE?**   15
   Story Ideas from Aardvark to Zebra

5. **MORE STORIES BEHIND THE STORIES**   20
   Peter Z. Cohen, Jamie Gilson, Lila Perl, and Irene Bennett Brown

6. **WHAT WOULD HAPPEN IF?**   24
   Ideas to Play With on Paper and on Stage

7. **MORE STORIES BEHIND THE STORIES**   37
   William Sleator, Dorothy Francis, Patricia Reilly Giff, Marjorie Weinman Sharmat, and Berniece Rabe

8. **WHY?**   40
   Writing to Discover

9. **MORE STORIES BEHIND THE STORIES**   51
   Dean Hughes, C.S. Adler, Ellen Conford,
   and Dana Brookins

10. **THE IDEAS INSIDE YOUR HEAD**   55
    A Journal to Remember

11. **MORE STORIES BEHIND THE STORIES**   61
    David Harrison, Patricia Calvert, Robert C.
    Lee, and Mary Frances Shura

12. **THREE STEPS TO A STORY**   64
    Choosing Characters, Problems, and
    Solutions

13. **MORE STORIES BEHIND THE STORIES**   71
    Kristi Holl, Robert Kimmel Smith, Robert
    Burch, and David Melton

14. **A DOZEN GRAINS OF SAND**   74
    Ideas in Search of a Writer

15. **MORE BOOKS FOR YOUNG WRITERS**   80

INDEX   84

ABOUT THE AUTHOR   88

WHERE DO
YOU GET
YOUR IDEAS?

1

WHERE DO IDEAS COME FROM?

"Where do writers get their ideas?" people often ask me. "Where do you get your ideas?" they want to know.

It sounds as if there might be a secret place, one only writers know about, where ideas roam wild like horses. All we writers have to do is round them up, lasso one, and lead it home.

Or perhaps there's a shop somewhere with a clever little shopkeeper who piles the shelves high with ideas. New ideas, attractively displayed and very expensive. Slightly used ideas, tossed aside and on sale. Worn-out ideas in the basement, three for the price of one.

Maybe there's an Idea of the Month Club that only writers belong to, with a huge catalog packed full of ideas for us to pick and choose.

What about an Idea Delivery Service? Are fresh ideas tossed on our porches each morning along with the *Daily News*?

No. None of those places or shops or clubs or services is needed. The truth is, ideas are everywhere all the time. It's a wonder we can find room to walk down the street,

1

the world is so chock full of ideas. Most of the time, though, we simply don't notice they're there.

It's a lot like radio waves. Radio waves travel around us constantly, zipping right past our ears day and night. But we don't hear them unless we have a receiver—that is, a radio. Radios are made to pick up radio signals, but even they can't do it if their power isn't turned on. Brains are made to pick up idea signals, but, again, they can't do it unless their power is turned on.

So, how do you turn on your brain's idea receiver?

Different writers have different ways. Some like to sit quietly in a park or restaurant or shopping mall and observe everything that's going on around them. Sooner or later, something or someone especially interesting catches their eye, and they've found a new idea to write about.

Others like to stay home alone and daydream about faraway places and adventures that can take place only in their imaginations. One adventure seems more exciting than all the others, and a brand-new story has begun.

Still other writers like to travel, or pull ideas out of their memories, or read until a new idea occurs to them.

The alternate chapters of this book are called "Stories Behind the Stories," or "More Stories Behind the Stories." In these chapters well-known authors tell how some of their popular tales came to be. As you'll see, no two stories got started in quite the same way, not even two stories by the same author.

As for me, I've found three questions that help bring new ideas to my mind:

The first is, How many ways can this be done?

The second is, What would happen if?

And the third is, simply, Why?

2

HOW MANY WAYS CAN THIS BE DONE?

Waking Up to Poetry

I discovered this question some time ago in my daughter's bedroom. That's an odd place to discover a question, but there it was!

Emily's bedroom in the house where we lived at that time was tiny. It had barely enough space for her bed, a closet, and a chest of drawers. There was only one small window. Outside of that window was a giant sweetgum tree whose leaves and branches completely blocked out the view.

One morning, while Emily was at school, I went into that room to clean it, and the thought suddenly struck me: What a boring room this is! What must it be like, I wondered, to wake up in this room day after day with the same old bed, the same old closet, the same old chest of drawers, the same old window, and the same old tree?

Then I got to thinking: Is it really always the same? How many different ways can you wake up in the morning, even if you are in the same old room?

You can wake up hungry.

You can wake up sick.

You can wake up on your birthday.
You can wake up after a nightmare.
You can wake up to the year's first snow.
You can wake up still sleepy.
On and on I went, until I'd come up with thirty-two different ways to wake up. I'm sure there are more, but thirty-two seemed quite enough for the moment. I wrote them all down, and I began to create poems for each of them.

Not all of the poems worked out. Not all ideas are good! But here are a few of my favorites:
This one's for those chilly mornings when you just don't want to put your feet down on that ice-cold floor.

● JUST ONE MORE ●

Just one more deep wide wonderful yawn.
Just one more shivery stretch.
Please?
Just one more snatch-of-dream,
    slumber-sneaking doze.
Just one more snuggle in my quilt?
I'll get up.
I really will.
After just one more—
    After just—
    After one—
I'll get up.

Here's a nicer way to wake up.

● HOTCAKES FOR BREAKFAST ●

Sweet and heavy,
like a slow-moving dream,
comes the smell of crackling bacon
and hot cocoa steam
to rouse up dreamers
on a frosty day
with hotcakes for breakfast
to chase chills away.
Sleepy eyes light
as thick syrup flows:
sweet
  and heavy
    and slowly
      it goes.

Has anything like this ever happened to you?

● SURPRISE! ●

Jump up, sleepyhead!
Grab your skirt
and socks and shirt.
Yank that zipper,
pull that bow,
dash into the hall
and what do you know?

Mom and Dad
are still tucked in.
Brother greets you
with a grin:
"Thought I'd stop you
on your way
to school
because
it's Saturday!"

I wrote this one to cheer up my son, but Emily needed it, too, when she woke up sick a few days later!

● SLY AS A POX ●

Benjamin A.
is sickly today;
he has to stay
home from school.

Small spots of red
on his arms and his head
remind us that bed
is the rule.

Each spot's an itch
that makes Benjy twitch!
He doesn't know which
way to wiggle.

Yet, winking his eye,
he asks by and by
a question so wry
he must giggle:

*"The comfort is small,
but children who fall
to chicken pox soon find
they're mild pox.*

*But can you suppose
the sadness of those
poor chickens that suffer
from child pox?"*

Some alarm clocks bark!

● PEPPER, I SAID I'M SLEEPING ●

*What good's a pillow
over your head
when your dog's fat paw
flips it right off the bed?*

Pepper, I said I'm sleeping.

*What good's a blanket
wrapped around twice
when your dog's poky nose
is colder than ice?*

Pepper, I said I'm sleeping!

*What good's pretending
with snoring and wheezing
when your dog's tail tickles
till you can't stop sneezing?*

Pepper, I guess I'm awake now.

How many different ways can you think of to wake up?
Can you beat my record of thirty-two?

Let's get started. Let's write poetry right now.

1. Think about waking up on any old day at all. As you
do, complete these lines:

I see...
I hear ....
I taste ....
I smell ....
I feel ....
I think ....

2. Read over what you've written. Is everything in the
right order? Close your eyes for a moment and really
imagine waking up. What happens first? A sound? A
thought? A smell?

Try writing a poem this way, now:

First I ....
Then I ....

9

Next I ....

And I ....

When I ....

Then I ....

3. You don't need to worry about rhyme, if you don't want to. Not all poets use it. What you do need to use, though, are the best words you can find to describe what's going on. The best words aren't always the first to come to mind. Go over your poems and make them stronger if you can.

4. Do you like one poem better than the other? If so, give it a title. If you like both, add a title to each.

5. Now you can get to work remembering not just any old day, but particular days, one at a time. Good days and bad. Cold days and hot. Weekdays and holidays and important days of all kinds. Ordinary days, too.

Keep in mind the sights, sounds, smells, tastes, feelings, and thoughts that are special to each day. Notice that "Hotcakes for Breakfast" is mainly about smells and tastes. Can you write a poem entirely about smells and tastes? How about one that's all about sounds?

There are as many ways to write about days as there are days to remember!

● ● ●

"How many ways can this be done?" The question helps find poetry ideas, but what else can it do? We'll find out in chapter 4, after a glimpse of some "Stories Behind the Stories."

3

STORIES BEHIND THE STORIES

Ideas, I think, come from two places. Outside—that is, everything we see and do, and everything that happens to us. And inside—when our own special imagination starts mixing with the outside.

Some years ago, my beloved orange cat, Solomon, gave me the idea for a book called *Time Cat*. Solomon had a way of suddenly appearing in my workroom, then disappearing before I noticed that he had gone. This made me pretend that he was magically able to visit any of his nine lives whenever he felt like it. *Time Cat* was my first fantasy for young people and I have Solomon to thank for it.

Lloyd Alexander,
*also author of **Westmark***
*and **The Prydain Chronicles***

● ● ●

I was sitting with a friend in the Boston Public Garden. It was early evening, and they were just closing up the Swan Boats. While I watched, they began to secure them

with a complicated set of chains and padlocks. I found myself wondering why on earth they had to do that. Who would steal an enormous, unwieldy, foolish-looking boat built in the shape of a swan?

My imagination began to take over. A bank robber, I fantasized: Here he comes, making his getaway with a satchel full of unmarked bills, and he leaps onto a Swan Boat and sails away. DUMB, I decided. He leaps onto a Swan Boat and sails away, around and around a small pond, and in the meantime forty-seven policemen encircle the pond, and so much for the great getaway.

Well, who would, then? I thought. And I decided: Of course. Kids. Teenagers. At night.

Why would they?

Well, by the time I walked home, about four blocks away, I had begun to put together the entire plot for the book which was eventually titled *Taking Care of Terrific*.

Lois Lowry,
*also author of **Anastasia Krupnik***
*and **Autumn Street***

● ● ●

When I first heard the term *divine inspiration,* I imagined a messenger from heaven knocking at a writer's door every morning and handing her/him a list of ideas. Now I know from many days of sitting in front of the typewriter and a blank piece of paper that ideas simmer around in the back of my mind until they're ready to boil over. If the feeling is strong enough, a book may evolve. Or maybe not. But when something happens and a year later I'm holding a new novel in my hand, I want to jump up and down, throw confetti, and stop everyone on the street and say, Look what I've done.

When one of my daughters was in the sixth grade, a nasty girl moved into town and began making her life miserable at school. I had a choice. I could either blow her house up or write a book about peer pressure in the classroom. When *The Iceberg and Its Shadow* came out, I received many letters from young people who asked, How did you know this happened to me?

Jan Greenberg,
*also author of **The Pig-Out Blues***
*and **No Dragons to Slay***

● ● ●

Sometimes it's simply a word that first fascinates, then claims me for its own. That's how Muggles in *The Gammage Cup* was born. She got her start from *muddle,* a word which accidentally landed in my head one day and circled and bumped around there until it grew into a full-fledged character, a (seemingly) muddled, humble sort of Minnipin, a Candy Maker. In *The Firelings,* the character Mole Star owes his being (with a slight change in pronunciation) to a "Please do not disturb" sign in a Madrid hotel room, which read—in Spanish, of course— *"Favor no molestar."* I knew instantly that Mole Star was mine.

Carol Kendall,
also author of **Sweet and Sour** *and*
Haunting Tales from Japan

● ● ●

HOW MANY DIFFERENT WAYS CAN ANYTHING BE DONE?

Story Ideas from Aardvark to Zebra

1. Suppose I asked you to write about an animal. How many different animals could you think of?

Dog,
cat,
canary,
horse,
cow,
elephant,
zebra,
snake,
monkey,
toad,
gnu,
tiger,
bear,
lion,
bat,
giraffe,
aardvark,
armadillo,

> buffalo,
>> donkey,
>>> rabbit,
>>>> pig,
>>>>> gerbil,
>>>>>> spider,
>>>>>>> lizard.

And that's hardly all.

You could write a story about each of these animals, and no two of your stories would be alike. Spiders and giraffes simply don't have the same adventures. An aardvark's day is nothing like a zebra's. Each animal's way of life presents a new idea for a story.

2. Suppose I put a limit on your story and said you had to write about a dog. How many different dogs could you think of?

German shepherd,
Chihuahua,
Shih Tzu,
poodle,
dachshund,

> Great Dane,
> greyhound,
> Doberman pinscher,
> Pekingese,
> schnauzer,

>> beagle,
>> Labrador retriever,
>> bulldog,
>> cocker spaniel,
>> St. Bernard.

To name just a few.

And don't forget the mutts: brown mutts, white mutts, gray mutts, brown mutts with white spots, white mutts with black spots, big mutts, small mutts, fat mutts and thin mutts.

Then, of course, there's my dog, your dog, your friend's dog, and your cousin's dog. (Not to mention the dog who keeps turning over everybody's trash can.)

Each and every dog has a different story to tell. A Chihuahua's story will never be a Great Dane's story. A mutt's life is rarely like a poodle's. Then, again, what about a mutt whose owner treats her like a prized poodle? Now there's another idea for a story!

3. What if I made the rules even stricter and said you had to write about one particular dog: a German shepherd named King. How many different adventures could you think of for that one dog?

He could get lost and have to find his way home.

He could be the leader of a pack of wild dogs.

He might get hurt—hit by a car, maybe, or accidentally shot by a hunter,
or maybe he gets dognapped.
He might get in trouble by biting someone.
Or he might save someone's life—a drowning victim,
or someone trapped in a fire,
or lost in a blizzard.
(How many different ways can a dog save lives?)
He could win first prize in a dog show.
He could work as a police dog,
or a Seeing Eye dog,
or a circus dog,
or a movie star,
or he could do something else entirely.

4. If we added up all the dogs we could think of and all the adventures they might have and all the other kinds of animals we could think of and all the adventures they might have, we would have so many ideas to write about, we could share them with an army of writers and still never run out.

And that's just animal stories . . .

How many different uses can you think of for a paper bag?

How many different ways can you think of to travel?

How many different faces can you make—and what do they mean?

How many different kinds of food do you like?

How many different words can you use to describe yourself?

How many different things can you do to have fun?

How many different uses can you think of for your hands?

How many different people do you meet in a day?

How many different things can you find around you that are red?

And—

how many different questions like these can you think of?

How many of your answers are ideas you'd like to write a story about? Or a poem? Or a play?

Not all of them, of course. But a writer needs only one at a time to get started.

● ● ●

We'll get back to work in chapter 6, but first, more "Stories Behind the Stories," just for the fun of it.

5

MORE STORIES BEHIND THE STORIES

While I was at the University of Wyoming, I had an after-hours horse who was a pleasure under the saddle, but a demon to catch if loose. In a corral, he had to be roped; out on pasture, I had to keep him haltered to an auto tire casing that he dragged as he grazed. There's a lot of open country around Laramie, and twice, eight or ten miles from town, we were whited-out by sudden snowstorms. I could scarcely see his ears, but by relaxing the reins and letting the horse have his head, I arrived safely home. But what, I thought, if he were to get loose from me in such a situation? I wrote *Morena* rather in self-defense, as a way of imagining in advance what to be prepared for should such an emergency come.

Peter Z. Cohen,
*also author of **Calm Horse,***
Wild Night
*and **Muskie Hook***

● ● ●

I visit schools, sometimes for several days at a stretch, taking notes—lots of notes—about what the room looks like, what the kids are doing and saying. I also teach writing workshops to sixth graders, and learn, in that way, what kids are thinking about. Watching and listening, that's how I get my ideas.

Though I've only done it a couple of times, I like starting with titles that sum up the story, capsulize it. While out in the car one morning, I thought of *The Invincible Rubber Band*, a story of a group of boys who

shoot rubber bands. But it was soon clear that the teacher would just take them away and the story would be very short—and dull. Then I began to consider what kind of teacher you *might* be able to fool with rubber band shooting, and decided on a brand-new substitute teacher.

It occurred to me that kids did more than shoot rubber bands to get subs. And, that same morning, I thought of the title that I used, *Thirteen Ways to Sink a Sub*. And in the book, they didn't even shoot rubber bands, but were generally more inventive. It was subs who told me the sub sinkers, not the kids.

Jamie Gilson,
also author of **Dial Leroy Rupert, D.J.**
and **Do Bananas Chew Gum?**

● ● ●

Fat Glenda, based on a person I knew (but changed by my own imagination), was one of my best story ideas. When she first appeared in *Me and Fat Glenda*, readers from all over the country began to write me letters about her. They wanted to know if she'd lost weight after the story ended. They sent me reducing diets and exercise programs for her. It wasn't just Glenda's fatness that made people care. She was a sympathetic character who seemed to touch something hidden in all of us.

Lila Perl,
also author of **Hey, Remember Fat Glenda?**
and **Fat Glenda's Summer Romance**

● ● ●

Curiosity can result in an idea for a book. For example, I was curious to know what it was like to be a boy growing up in the time and place of my grandfather. I read a great deal about Missouri in the late 1880's and from the reading came the idea for my book *Run from a Scarecrow*.

In *Before the Lark,* I wanted to know how it feels to have an affliction one cannot help, and be shunned and ill-treated because of it. How does one deal with the torment at the hands of others? What does one do to overcome the problem and make a good life? Jocey Royal is an outcast because of facial disfigurement, a harelip, in the days before corrective surgery became common. By telling her story, I could show that injustice can be dealt with, and overcome, sometimes even gloriously.

Following an idea is to go exploring! It's great fun!

Irene Bennett Brown,
*also author of **Morning Glory Afternoon***
*and **Just Another Gorgeous Guy***

● ● ●

6

WHAT WOULD HAPPEN IF?

Ideas to Play with on Paper and on Stage

1. What would happen if a spaceship landed on earth and one of its creatures got left behind when it took off again?

That's the idea behind the movie *E.T.*

What would happen if there were a place where children never had to grow up?

That's the idea behind *Peter Pan*.

What would happen if a cyclone picked someone up and carried her off to a strange and wonderful place?

That's the idea behind *Dorothy and the Wizard of Oz*.

Have you ever wondered, What would happen if?

One of the nice things about writing is that once you've thought of the question, you can usually find out the answer. All you have to do is start writing—and you'll soon see what does happen.

Another nice thing about writing is that there are so many fascinating questions to ask. And there are even more fascinating answers than there are questions!

For instance, here's one question with many possible answers: What would happen if one of your classmates grew up—overnight?

He might not fit into his seat when he arrived at school. The water fountains would seem too low. Maybe no one would recognize him. Maybe the teacher would send him away—and then mark him absent!

What would happen if everybody in your class wrote a play about it? Would all the plays be the same?

Here are two scenes from the middle of such a play. It has a title, *A Big Day for Rufus*. But it has no beginning and no ending. Perhaps you can help finish it.

● A BIG DAY FOR RUFUS ●

Characters

> RUFUS GRIMBLETON, a schoolboy
> MOM GRIMBLETON, his mother
> DAD GRIMBLETON, his father
> MRS. BUSTLEBY, the school bus driver
> JO, Rufus's best friend
> OTHER CHILDREN

Scene 1

Setting: *The kitchen of the Grimbleton home. On stage are a table and three chairs. DAD GRIMBLETON is at the table, reading the newspaper. MOM GRIMBLE-TON is busily making and serving breakfast. RUFUS rushes onstage in pajamas several sizes too small for him.*

Rufus: My pajamas! My pajamas shrunk! In the middle of the night, they just shrunk! How can that be? Look at them. They hardly cover my elbows. They don't even reach my knees. Mom! Look at what happened to my pajamas!

Mom: (rushing over to RUFUS, in great alarm) Oh, Rufus, never mind about your pajamas. Look at what happened to *you!*

Rufus: Me? Nothing happened to me. It's the pajamas. They've shrunk. (He suddenly takes a good look at his mother.) Oh, my goodness, Mom! You've shrunk, too!

Mom: No, I haven't, Rufus. It's you. You've grown. You've grown up overnight. Dad always said you were getting too big for your britches, but this is ridiculous.

Rufus: (measuring himself up to his mother and realizing that he's taller than she is) Wow! I *have* grown, haven't I? Gee, Mom, I never noticed it before, but your hair's getting a little gray on top.

Mom: Never mind my hair. What are we going to do about you?

Rufus: I don't know. I haven't had much time to think about growing up. It's happened so fast.

Mom: Well, there's no time to think about it now. Morning is just no time for thinking. You have to get ready for school. Dad and I have to get to work. We'll just have to do our thinking later. (She shoos RUFUS offstage.) Go on. Get dressed. And hurry, or you'll miss your bus.

Rufus: (as he exits) Okay.

Mom: (getting the coffee pot and bringing it to DAD, who never comes out from behind his newspaper at the table) More coffee, Dear?

Dad: (Without lowering his paper, he pushes his coffee cup across the table toward her.) Uh-huh.

Mom: (pours coffee) There you go.

Dad: (without lowering paper) Thanks.

Rufus: (enters, still in his pajamas) Uh, Mom?

Mom: No nonsense, now, Rufus. Morning is no time for nonsense. You get dressed for school.

Rufus: But, Mom, what should I wear?

Mom: You know what to wear. It's all right there in your closet.

Rufus: Yes, but—

Mom: Rufus, you get dressed right this minute. I don't want to hear another word about it, is that clear? It's past eight o'clock already, do you realize that?

Rufus: Yes, Mom, whatever you say. (He exits.)
(MOM pours herself a cup of coffee and sits down at the table.)

Mom: (to DAD, who never puts down his paper) Anything in the news about that snowstorm we were supposed to get, Dear?

Dad: Uh-uh.

Mom: Have you seen any ads yet for that movie we've been wanting to see—*The Goldfish That Ate Dubuque?*

Dad: Uh-uh.

Mom: Any mention in there of children growing up overnight?

Dad: Uh-uh.

Mom: You're sure?

Dad: Uh-huh.

Mom: (thoughtfully) Hmmmmmm.
(RUFUS enters in clothes several sizes too small for him.)

Rufus: Well, here I am, I guess.

Mom: Good for you. (She jumps up from the table without really looking at him and brings him a bowl of cereal.) Now, sit down and eat your breakfast. (She exits hurriedly to get ready for work.)

Rufus: Okay. (He sits down and addresses DAD, who is still buried in the paper.) Good morning, Dad.

Dad: (without looking up) Morning, Son.

Rufus: Who won last night's game, Dad?

Dad: They did, Son.

Rufus: Oh. Too bad.

Dad: Uh-huh.

Rufus: Did Mom tell you what happened to me, Dad?

Dad: (still behind newspaper) Don't talk with your mouth full, Son.

Rufus: I'm not talking with my mouth full. This is my new voice.

Dad: (not really listening) Uh-huh.

Rufus: I'm all grown up.

Dad: Good for you, Son.

Rufus: I think I'm going to need some new clothes, Dad.

Dad: Not now, Son. Maybe tomorrow.

Rufus: Well, I can hardly breathe in these. I don't know if I can hold my breath till tomorrow.

Dad: (not really listening) Um-hmmmmmm. That's good. Keep up the good work, Son.

Rufus: (with a sigh) Oh, okay, Dad. Gee, I wonder what the other kids will say.

Mom: (re-enters hurriedly) Stop wondering, Rufus, and finish your breakfast. Morning is no time for wondering. You're going to be late for school. (to DAD) You'd better finish up, too, Dear. We've all got to be on our way.

Dad: Um-hmmmmmm. (Still reading the paper, he stands up and leans across the table to kiss MOM's cheek.)

Mom: Goodbye, Dear.

Dad: (still reading) Bye. Have a nice day. (He pats RUFUS on the cheek.) Goodbye, Rufus, be a good boy. (He starts to walk away.) And don't forget to shave. (He walks a little farther, then stops and finally drops the newspaper.) Don't forget to shave? Rufus! What's happened to you?

Rufus: Oh, it's nothing, Dad. I've just grown up. A little sooner than we expected. Overnight.

Dad: How? How did it happen?

Rufus: I don't know. It just did.

Dad: What are we going to do?

Mom: We're going to hurry up to work or we'll be late, that's what we're going to do. We'll just have to worry about Rufus later. Oh, these mornings! These mornings! Getting the three of us up and out of here is getting harder every day.

Dad: Are you sure I ought to go to work? I mean, will Rufus be all right? Maybe I should take the day off.

Mom: What good will that do?

Dad: I don't know. I just feel I ought to do *something*.

Rufus: You could lend me some clothes, Dad. I'm pretty uncomfortable like this.

Dad: (as he and MOM notice RUFUS's outfit for the first time) Oh, of course, Son. Anything you say. Anything you need. Just help yourself. What size shirt do you wear?

Rufus: I don't know, Dad.

Dad: No, of course not. I'm sorry. It's just . . . oh, my little boy. My little baby boy . . . is a man!

Rufus: Oh, that reminds me, Dad. May I borrow your razor?

Dad: Yes, of course. Oh, my goodness. I'm astonished!

Mom: (to DAD) Morning is no time for astonishment, Dear. Let's all meet here at dinnertime and be astonished. We'll have so much more time for it then.

Dad: Yes, yes, of course. Oh, my goodness gracious. (He starts for door, takes a look back at Rufus, and shakes his head in bewilderment.)

Rufus: Bye, Dad.

Dad: Goodbye . . . Son. (He exits.)

Mom: All right, Rufus. Don't just stand there. Go!

Rufus: Be ready in a minute, Mom. (He exits.)

Mom: (clearing the table) A minute is about all you have. If you miss the bus, you'll have to walk. I don't have time to drive you to school, you know that. Oh, why can't mornings start later in the day? In the evening, maybe, when we have more time to deal with them. (She hurries across the stage and looks out a window.) Oh, dear. Rufus, the bus is at the top of the hill. It's stopped. It's loading. It's starting up again. Hurry! Here it comes! It's here!

Rufus: (enters in his father's suit and tie) I'm ready. How do I look, Mom?

Mom: Like your own father!

Rufus: Great! (He kisses MOM on the cheek.) Bye, Mom.

Mom: Goodbye . . . Son. (RUFUS exits. MOM watches him go, then shakes her head sadly and exits in the opposite direction. The lights fade. End of scene.)

Scene 2

Setting: *The bus stop in front of the Grimbleton's house. This scene may be played in front of the closed curtain or on a bare stage. Several children enter from one direction; RUFUS enters from the opposite direction.*

Rufus: Hi, Susie. Hi, Rick. (The CHILDREN back away from him nervously.) Hey, you two, don't you recognize me? (JO enters.) Hi, Jo!

Jo: My mom told me never to talk to strangers. (She joins the other CHILDREN as far away from RUFUS as they can get.)

Rufus: I'm not a stranger.

Jo: You look pretty strange to me.

Rufus: It's *me*, Jo. It really is. It's *me*.

Jo: Watch it, mister. I know a little karate.

Rufus: Oh, Jo, you do not.

Jo: Do, too! I've seen all the movies. (MRS. BUSTLEBY and more CHILDREN shuffle in, lined up and moving in unison as if MRS. BUSTLEBY were driving a bus and the CHILDREN were passengers. They shuffle to a stop. JO rushes past MRS. BUSTLEBY and takes her place in the line of passengers.)

Jo: Mrs. Bustleby, just in the nick of time!

Mrs. Bustleby: I try to be prompt, Jo. (The CHILDREN who were waiting with JO race past RUFUS and MRS. BUSTLEBY and take their places as passengers.) No running, children. Take it easy, there.

Rufus: (approaching MRS. BUSTLEBY as if to follow the others) Good morning.

Mrs. Bustleby: And where do you think you're going, young man?

Rufus: To school.

Mrs. Bustleby: Well, you want the city bus, back on the corner over there. See the sign?

Rufus: But—

Mrs. Bustleby: Guess you're new around here, huh?

Rufus: But—

Mrs. Bustleby: Welcome to the neighborhood. Your bus will be along any minute now. It'll take you right to the high school.

Rufus: But you don't understand.

Mrs. Bustleby: Oh, sure, I do. I was the new kid on the block once myself. Well, I'd like to stay and chat with you, but I've got a schedule too, you know. The kids really depend on me, and I don't like to keep them waiting. Have a nice day, now. Don't miss your bus.

(MRS. BUSTLEBY and the CHILDREN— except RUFUS—shuffle offstage.)

Rufus: (watching them go, unhappily) But, but, but— oh, no! Now I'll have to run all the way to school. This is going to be a really weird day. (He trudges offstage in the direction of the "bus." The lights fade. End of scene.)

2. There it is: the middle of a play. What would happen if *you* wrote the opening and closing scenes?

What do you think will happen to Rufus now?

Will he become the star of his school's basketball team, or will he have to quit school and find a job?

Will he stay grown up, or will he suddenly grow down again?

And why do you suppose this has happened to him in the first place?

Is there a magician behind it,
or a witch's spell,
or creatures from outer space?
Could he have eaten something poisonous,
or breathed polluted air?
What if he's discovered an amazing secret formula?
Does he remember doing it? Does he remember drinking
it? Does he remember how to undo it?

Are his family and schoolmates involved? Are they in
danger? Can he save them? Can anyone save them?

3. Once you've decided how Rufus got into this mess, you might want to get together with some of your friends, assign the various parts, and act out possible scenes to add.

If you do the play just for your own enjoyment, you can act it out differently each time and not worry if it doesn't all make perfect sense. But if eventually you find you want to perform it for an audience, you're going to have to decide on one way to do it, then stick with that decision. And you'll need to polish your script and your performances until they glow.

After you've gone through each scene, talk it over. Are there lines and actions that need to be put in to make the story clearer? Are there parts that just waste time and should be left out? Will you need a narrator to tie scenes together?

Once the play starts to take shape, you might want to tape-record your rehearsals. Have the cast listen to the tapes once or twice before each new rehearsal begins. That way, nothing important will be left out the next time you run your scenes through.

You could write or type the whole script out, but it may be better not to. By listening to the tapes and repeating the scenes often enough, your actors will be memorizing as they go along.

You may—or may not—want to act the scenes in this chapter exactly as they're written. You may want to add or take out characters. Or change their names. Or choose a new title. That's entirely up to you. *A Big Day for Rufus* began as my idea, but when it's finished, it will be all yours.

7

MORE STORIES BEHIND THE STORIES

In science fiction, I find ideas in novels by other writers. This may sound like theft, but it is an accepted practice in the science-fiction community. If you are writing a book about time travel, for instance, you can't just go to the library and look up *Time Travel* in the encyclopedia or the physics section, because it doesn't exist. So to spark your imagination you read other science-fiction books about time travel and take off from there, changing the ideas and making them your own.

Sometimes kids suggest that dreams might be a source of ideas. And it is true that I got one idea for a book from a dream I had about two people who were having the same dream. The girl and the boy in *Into the Dream* hate each other in the beginning, but by the end of the book they have become best friends.

However, dreams are not really a great source of ideas, because you can't say to yourself, "I need an idea for a new book, so tonight I will go to sleep and have a dream

37

and write a book about that dream." Dreams just aren't that dependable.

William Sleator,
*also author of **Interstellar Pig***
*and **Fingers***

● ● ●

In my book *The Flint Hills Foal,* I drew on the character of my daughter, who loves horses, and on the character of her friend, who was afraid of horses, as well as the characters who were often seen around the stables. The situation I drew on involved the disappearance of a newborn foal. In my book, I fictionalized this situation and it was the mare rather than the foal that was missing. Consequently, the story concerns a young girl's attempt to raise a motherless foal.

Dorothy Francis,
*also author of **Captain Morgana Mason***
*and **The Warning***

● ● ●

I wrote *Fourth Grade Celebrity* about my own fourth-grade experiences. There really was a Secret Passageway behind my house, we really did dig up dead fish all summer long, and we wrote to a pen pal to say that my sister was dead! (She wasn't!)

Patricia Reilly Giff,
*also author of **The Winter Worm Business***
*and **Rat Teeth***

● ● ●

My Nate the Great series was inspired by my father, Nathan "Nate" Weinman. I wanted to name a character in a book after him. When I thought of Nate, I thought of *great*, and my series of ten (so far) books about the boy detective was born.

Marjorie Weinman Sharmat,
*also author of **The Son of the Slime Who Ate***
Cleveland
*and **I Saw Him First***

● ● ●

My books actually start with a feeling, good or bad. (Not an idea.) Then, I conjure up the image that is associated with that feeling. That's sort of like a snapshot of people in a given place. (Still not an idea.) Next I start rolling the image into action and my characters are in a motion picture in my mind. (Still not an idea.) Next I ask myself a few questions about just WHY those characters are acting the way they are. It gets my curiosity going. (An idea is about to come!) I begin to write down how these characters look and talk and some of the things I see them doing. I continue to wonder WHY they're doing it that way. My idea comes when I answer that WHY. Now, I've got a story going.

Berniece Rabe,
*author of **Rass***
*and **Margaret's Moves***

WHY?

Writing to Discover

Why is the sun brighter than the moon?

Why do stars twinkle?

Why are some people mean?

Why don't I have freckles?

Why do I sometimes feel sad when nothing bad has happened?

Why are some people smarter than others?

Why don't I like everybody the same?

There is no end to the number of questions that begin with "*Why?*" And every one of them can be the start of a good idea to write about.

Some of them require research: a visit to the library to read what the experts have to say on the subject.

Others require talking to the people involved to find out what they think about the problem and what they intend to do about it.

Still others require a different kind of research—a long, hard look into our own minds and imaginations to see if we can figure out the answer for ourselves.

I once knew a student, a fifth grader, who always

insulted people. She never gave anyone a chance to be nice to her. Before they could even try, she'd say something nasty. Her classmates quickly learned to leave her alone. Everyone she met soon decided to stay out of her way.

Why does she do that? I wondered. It doesn't make her happy. In fact, she seems quite lonely and sad. I never could get her to talk it over with me.

Years later, I still wondered about that girl, and I still had no answer to my question, so I decided to write a story about her. Just for fun, I turned her into a princess, a very haughty princess. And I made her insults come out in rhyme. But behind the fun, there was still that serious question, Why does she do it?

The more I wrote about her, the more I understood, until in one scene, the answer finally popped out of the princess's mouth. Here is that story. See if you can find out *why*.

● THE INSULTING PRINCESS ●

Once there was a princess named Greta, who was famous throughout the world.

Famous for what? you might well ask. Who'd give a fig for this stiff and scowling creature?

Well, Greta was famous for her insults.

The king and queen lured one royal suitor after another to the palace. They promised half their kingdom to anyone who could cure Greta of her insulting habit.

But when the Knight of Knoodle offered Greta a rose, she said, "This rose you've brought will come in handy— for hiding your nose, which is really a dandy."

The knight left, rather quickly.

When the Duke of Cuke asked Greta for her hand in marriage, she said, "As a groom, you'll never do, but fat as you are, you'd make a fine stew."

The duke fled.

When the Earl of Vinegar came to call, Greta announced, "Tall as a tower, thin as a post—I wouldn't use you to spread jam on my toast."

The earl vanished.

"Someone must cure Greta," the king and queen cried.

"Cure Greta?" the villagers exclaimed. "Whatever happened to the easy stuff like slaying dragons? Or ridding the land of giants? Cure Greta? Impossible!"

One day a newcomer arrived in the village. His name was Alfred, and he was a baker. He had found a kitten wandering all alone on the road.

"Has anyone lost this kitten?" Alfred asked everyone he met. No one claimed it.

Alfred tucked the kitten into his apron pocket. Door to

door he went, knocking and asking, asking and knocking, until he happened to arrive at the palace gate.

There he met the king and queen, fretting, as usual, over Greta. Alfred bowed.

"Your Majesties," he said, noticing their unhappiness. "Have you lost a kitten?"

"We have not," replied the king, glumly.

"Then would you like to have a kitten?" asked Alfred.

"We would not," sighed the queen. "The last thing in the world we need is a kitten."

"Oh?" said Alfred. "Then what's the first thing you need in the world?"

"A cure for Greta," said the king and the queen together. And they poured out the whole sad story of Greta and her insulting habit.

"Knights, earls, and dukes have tried to cure her," said the king, shaking his head in dismay.

"And all have failed," said the queen, wiping a tear from her royal eye.

Before Alfred could say a word, the king clapped his hands excitedly. "A prince could do it," he cried. "Princes always can."

"Must it be a prince?" asked Alfred.

"Of course!" agreed the queen. "Who cured the princess who couldn't laugh? And who cured the princess who couldn't cry? And who woke Sleeping Beauty with a kiss? It always has been, always is, and always will be a prince."

"Couldn't it, every now and then, be an ordinary person?" asked Alfred. "Couldn't it, maybe just once, perhaps, be a baker like me?"

"Certainly not," said the king.

"But why?" asked Alfred.

"Because a princess would have nothing to do with an ordinary person like you," said the queen, with a haughty sniff. "Come to think of it, neither should we. Goodbye."

And off went the king and queen to begin their search for a prince.

Alfred was furious.

"A prince, indeed," he fumed at the kitten, who was the only one left to listen. "Nothing to do with an ordinary person like me? Ridiculous!"

"Yes, you are," said a voice. "Even from afar."

Alfred quickly tucked the kitten back into his pocket. Then he looked up to see a face scowling at him from behind a rosebush prickly with thorns. Although he had never seen that face before in his life, he knew it could belong to only one person—

Princess Greta.

And she had spoken to him!

"Good day, Your Highness," he called through the iron bars of the fence.

"You might think it good if your head were of wood," Greta called back.

Again, she spoke! Nothing very nice, of course, but wasn't she treating him exactly as she treated dukes and earls and knights? Possibly princes, too.

Alfred smiled pleasantly. "Yes, I suppose one might," he said, "if one could think at all with a wooden head. I don't know anything about that. But an ordinary head like my own definitely finds it good. Of that much, I am quite sure."

Was that the sort of thing a prince would say? Alfred wondered. Never mind. He had said it, and it would have to stay said.

Alfred put his hand in his apron pocket and nervously stroked the kitten. "I have something here you might like," he told Greta.

"To be perfectly blunt, you have nothing I'd want," Greta told him.

"Of course you don't want it," Alfred agreed. "How could you, when you don't even know what it is?"

Greta stiffened and scowled with all her might. "What is wrong with you?" she cried. "Why don't you get insulted and run away like all the others?"

"Insulted by what?" asked Alfred.

"By my words!" Greta roared.

"Oh, those!" Alfred replied. "Oh, well, I'm terribly sorry if I've disappointed you, but it takes two to make an insult. One to give and one to receive. If I am not insulted by your words, they are not insults. And I like myself. I think I'm nice. Nothing you can say will change my mind."

"Oh, no?" said Greta. "Get out of my sight, you blithering blight!"

"You may shriek and you may bray; as for me, I plan to stay," said Alfred.

"Insult a princess, you loitering loon? I'll have your head on a platter by noon!" snapped Greta.

"You don't scare me, and you'll never make queen. You're far too haughty and you're far too mean," chanted Alfred.

Greta stormed over to the iron fence. "You nattering nitwit!" she shrieked.

45

Alfred faced her, toe to toe. "You scowling screech owl!" he said.

Soon they were nose to nose.

"You lummox."

"You lunkhead."

"You lizard."

"You lout."

Eyebrow to eyebrow!

"You artichoke."

"You alleycat."

"You bumbler."

"You boor."

"You coward."

"You cad."

Lash to lash!

"Dummy."

"Dimwit."

"Elephant."

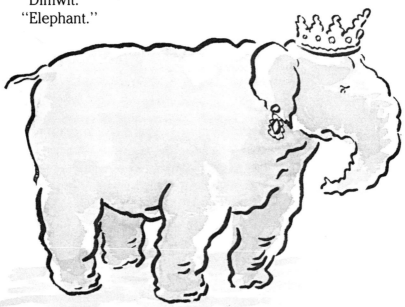

"Eel."
"Fleabite."
"Flibbertygibbet."
"Gorilla."
"Goon."
"Inkblot."
"Icicle."
"Jughead."
"Jerk."
"Killjoy."
"Kumquat."
"Laughingstock."
"Liverwurst."
"Monster."
"Misfit."
"Nincompoop."
"Nerd."
"Onion."

"Octopus."

"Pimple."

"Pig."

"Quagmire."

"Quack."

"Ragamuffin."

"Rapscallion."

"Simpleton."

"Sourpuss."

"Turtlehead."

"Toad."

"Upstart."

"Undertow."

"Weasel."

"Weed."

"Xyloid."

"Xenophobe."

"Yahoo."

"Yegg."

"Zany."

"Zip."

What next? They were out of breath, out of words, out of insults! Together they gasped helplessly, "You . . . you . . . you . . . you . . . "

"Meow," said the kitten.

"You meow?" said Greta. And she and Alfred burst out laughing.

The kitten leaped from Alfred's pocket to Greta's arms.

"I've never met anyone like you before," Greta told Alfred.

"I'm not surprised," said Alfred, "stuck away in a drafty old palace all by yourself."

"I'm not all by myself," said Greta. "I have my Royal Parents and my Royal Tutor and my Royal Athletic Coach and my Royal Dance Master and my Royal Lady-in-waiting and—"

"All very nice, I'm sure," interrupted Alfred, "but do you have a friend?"

"A friend?" echoed Greta. "No. No, I don't."

"You do now," said Alfred. "I like you."

"You do?" gasped Greta. "Are you sure? Oh, I've been so afraid no one ever would."

Suddenly, she stopped short and held the kitten closer.

"That's why I insult people, isn't it?" she said. "Because I'm afraid they'll insult me first."

"What if they do?" asked Alfred.

"It would hurt my feelings," said Greta.

"Only if you believed them," Alfred told her. "It takes two to make an insult, remember? My insults didn't hurt your feelings."

"That's true," Greta admitted. "They made me laugh."

"Insults are just silly old words—if you like yourself."

"Maybe I'm beginning to," said Greta.

And the kitten in her arms began to purr.

When the king and queen returned from their world-wide search, they were disappointed. No prince on earth would risk Greta's insults. They were also shocked. Alfred and the kitten were dining with Greta in the Royal Palace!

"How dare you?" the king shouted at Alfred.

But Greta cut him short. "I'm cured!" she announced.

"Without a Royal Prince?" asked the Queen. "How is that possible?"

"With a Royal Friend," Greta informed her. "And a Royal Cat."

"And a bit of laughter," Alfred added.
And that was that.

● ● ●

Why do people insult each other? Often because they don't feel good about themselves.

And why does it always have to be a prince? It doesn't. Not with a princess like Greta, who treats royalty like ordinary people, and ordinary people no better.

This story began and ended with my asking *why* and discovering the answer to my own question. But the other two questions we have discussed played important parts, too. What would happen if . . . ? made Greta a princess and Alfred a simple baker. It also tucked the kitten into Alfred's apron pocket. How many different ways can this be done? brought on the insults—and got them to rhyme.

What makes you wonder *why?*
Why don't you try writing about it?
How many different ways could you do it?
What would happen if you did?

MORE STORIES BEHIND THE STORIES

Have you ever noticed that when you're shopping for a new pair of shoes you become very aware, temporarily, of everyone's shoes? You notice shoes in stores and on people's feet, and you simply think about shoes more than usual. That's similar to what happens to me as a writer. I'm always shopping . . . for ideas.

I took a group of Boy Scouts on an outing once, and one of the boys in my car saw an older man walking down the street. The boy leaned out the window and yelled, "Hey, Gramps," which all the scouts found quite funny. I asked them what was so funny, but they didn't know. I asked them how they would feel if someone yelled at their grandfathers that way. They still had no answer. I started to wonder why young people, at times, are so cruel to older people. It seemed to me that a gap of understanding was the problem. The idea occurred to me to write a story about a boy and an older man who become friends and discover that their needs, problems, and feelings are not very different. The book is called *Switching Tracks*.

Dean Hughes,
also author of **Honestly, Myron** *and*
Nutty for President

● ● ●

Good-bye, Pink Pig . . . is a story based on something I own that I love, in this case, my shelf of miniatures. I imagined how it would be if some of those miniatures were alive and asked myself what kind of world they would live in and how they would relate to each other. Then I imagined a little girl who could enter that world, and made my special favorite, the rose quartz pig, the little girl's friend. Of course, there had to be a problem, because every story has one. So I decided that the wizard was casting evil spells in the miniature world. As for the girl, her mother didn't think much of her, and she was alone too much, and those were her problems until worse happened.

Split Sisters . . . began when I saw a pair of sisters who seemed closer to each other than best friends. Being an only child, I envied their warm relationship and started wondering about it. Would anything ever separate them? Well, a divorce might, if each parent decided to take one child. The younger sister was a funny kid. What could she do to keep from being separated from the older sister she adored? Answering my own questions is often the way I build up the framework of a story.

C.S. Adler,
also author of **The Magic of The Glits**
and **Carly's Buck**

● ● ●

It's hard to describe how an idea for a book comes to me. Some books just happen, and I never know how I thought them up. Some books were inspired by hearing an interesting name and then imagining what a character with that name would be like. I actually dreamed two of my books while I was asleep: *Lenny Kendall, Smart Aleck* and *To All My Fans, with Love, from Silvie*. The dreams were so real and so complete, that when I woke up I felt they were stories I had to write.

Only one of my books, *Hail, Hail, Camp Timberwood*, is entirely based on my own experiences. The rest are mostly made up, although some of the things I write about did happen to me.

Ellen Conford,
also author of **And This Is Laura**
and **Why Me?**

● ● ●

Everything I experience gets tucked into my memory file. If I see a curious looking person, *zap!* in goes that person. If I hear an interesting tidbit of conversation, *phoop!* in it goes. Then one day a lot of these tidbits of this and that all crowd into my conscious mind and cry, Hey, here we are. Get us down on paper; we're ready to become a book.

Once, in New York City, I saw a woman dressed in a black velvet evening gown, with rhinestone earrings, bracelet, necklaces, and a tiara. But she carried a green trash sack and rummaged in trash barrels; she was a bag lady. Another time, in Los Angeles, I passed a spooky alley at dusk. Its shadows stayed with me. Also in my memory file was my younger brother who, at age nine, often wore a strange outfit: a black raincoat, a World War One flying helmet with huge goggles, and our father's World War Two combat boots. That outfit, the elegant bag lady, and the spooky alley provided me with background material for a mystery novel called *Who Killed Sack Annie?*

Dana Brookins,
*also author of **Alone in Wolf Hollow***
*and **Rico's Cat***

● ● ●

10

THE IDEAS INSIDE YOUR HEAD

A Journal to Remember

It's been said that to duplicate the functions of one human brain would require a computer the size of six city blocks. Imagine all the writing ideas that would hold!

The truth is you do have a great deal to write about already tucked away in your own head. How do you get to it? Once more, by asking questions. How do you keep track of it all? By keeping a journal.

This is a special kind of journal. It is not arranged by dates. If you miss a day, or a week, or a month, you won't mess up the whole book. It is not one of those diaries with a few printed lines for each day, either, where the dull days look empty and the exciting days have to be squished in.

This journal is arranged by questions. You can answer them as often as you like and whenever you please. Use a loose-leaf notebook so pages can be added as you need them. You might want to put each question on a divider, followed by its pages of answers. However you arrange your journal, be sure to allow a separate section for each question.

Most important, write your responses as completely as you can. You may not develop these ideas into stories, plays, or poems for quite a while. When that day comes, though, you'll want to be able to look back at your journal entries, understand them, and remember exactly what you were writing about and how you felt about it at the time. Absolute neatness doesn't count, but completeness definitely does.

Here are seven questions to get your journal started:
1. Whom do I know?
2. What are the milestones of my life?
3. Where have I been?
4. What's wrong with my life?
5. What do I want?
6. What would happen if . . . ?
7. Why . . . ?

On the following pages, I've suggested the kinds of things you might want to enter in response to each question. Take your time. Don't try to answer a question all at once. There's no need to deal with every question every time you write. As the days go by, you'll think of more and more to add to your answers—a little bit here, a lot there, nothing for now somewhere else. That's why you'll need a loose-leaf notebook, one question to each section, and lots of blank paper.

1. *Whom do I know?*

Start with your family. You might even want to ask your parents and grandparents about their parents and grandparents. They're all a part of you. Move on to your friends, then add teachers, storekeepers, doctors, and anybody else you can think of.

If you like, you can add famous people, too, television and movie stars, musicians, politicians. You may not know them personally, but you can certainly describe them from what you've seen and heard and read. They, too, are part of you and your life.

Describe each person as carefully as you can: looks, personality, history, likes, dislikes. These people may find themselves in your stories someday. Or you might combine traits from two or three of them—one person's hair, another's sense of humor, a third's talent—to create a brand-new person.

2. *What are the milestones of my life?*

Think back as far as you can. Ask your parents for details if you need to. Describe the best and the worst of all the days of your life. The highs and the lows. The awards and the failures. The illnesses and the perfect days.

You'll have a lot more to add to this section as time goes on. And you never know which—a wonderful piece of luck or a terrible disaster—will be the idea for a story.

Be sure to include as much detail as you can recall. Remember the senses we used in the waking-up poems: taste, touch, smell, sight, and sound. They're important whenever you write.

3. *Where have I been?*

Try to pull out of your memory some of the many, many places you've been. What have you heard, seen, smelled, tasted, touched, and felt there?

Describe your major travels and the places you've lived, but don't forget the little scenes that have stuck with you—a classroom where you were especially happy, a dentist's office where you were worried or scared, the backstage area where you waited nervously to go on stage before a performance.

These may be the settings in which your stories take place someday. Your characters will walk in your footsteps.

4. *What's wrong with my life?*
Past, present, and future problems. Little annoyances. Serious troubles.

Here's the perfect place to complain, and gripe, moan, groan, whine, and howl. And no one can stop you!

In the next chapter, you'll learn that problems make stories. You can give your characters some of your problems, so lay in a good supply.

5. *What do I want?*
Here's the perfect place to dream.

Start with simple needs, like a softer pillow on your bed, and go on to complicated wishes and hopes, such as world peace. Realistic wants. Fantastic wants. Possible wants. Impossible wants. They're all wanted here.

If you could have everything, what would that everything include? A pet parakeet—or a pet Pegasus? One of each? If you want it, you can have it—in your imagination and in your writing.

6. *What would happen if . . . ?*
and

7. *Why . . . ?*
The questions for these last two sections should be familiar to you by now. Whenever you get a chance, see how many different ways you can complete each of them. Some will be silly. Others will be serious. Either way,

you're bound to come up with a few ideas you'll someday use in your writing.

If some of these questions don't appeal to you, leave them out. If you think of other questions you'd rather use, add them on. This is your journal, all about you. Enjoy yourself!

11

MORE STORIES BEHIND THE STORIES

Ideas have come from items in the news; a fragment of conversation, even a few words overheard; silly-tired thoughts that come late at night; indigestion, headaches or other pains or pressures can sometimes produce unexpected spurts of imagination . . .

Monster! Monster! originated from a news clipping about a woman who lived in Kansas. Returning home from lunch one day, she passed a hippopotamus standing beside the road. She made the news around the nation and I borrowed her problem for a book idea. I've tried a number of times to find that lady and send her a copy of the book she inspired, but she must have moved away.

David Harrison,
*also author of **The Book of Giant Stories***
*and **Wake Up, Sun!***

● ● ●

Many of my stories come from tales that my mother used to tell about her growing up years—she had nine brothers and sisters, so there were lots of stories! Pieces of some of my stories come from experiences that I had myself as I grew up in a very isolated community in central Montana. My school contained two children, my brother and me, and our mother was the teacher.

Many years ago, I read an article in *Time* magazine about a tribe of ancient people in the Zagros Mountains of Persia. These people were horse lovers and fashioned for their mounts a variety of trappings made out of bronze and iron. For some reason (no one knows why) these people were driven out of their mountains, and, as they left, they buried all their unique horse trappings—bridles and harnesses, bits, spurs, saddle rings, statues, etc. I told myself that someday I would write a story that would have something to do with those ancient people and their customs—and I did, twenty-eight years later, in a book called *The Stone Pony.*

Patricia Calvert,
*also author of **The Money Creek Mare***
*and **The Snowbird***

● ● ●

My oldest son, Rob, was the smallest boy in his high school class. He loved sports but the coaches weren't interested in him because he was so small. Finally the track coach let him run and he met with some success. This gave me the idea for *It's a Mile from Here to Glory,* a story about a little guy who turns out to be a great runner.

Robert C. Lee,
*also author of **The Summer of the Green Star***
*and **Timequake***

● ● ●

An idea is only a germ—never a book. It has to hang there in my mind until other thoughts and places gather around it. When the book is ready—it demands to be written!

Chester was the generic great kid I kept seeing all over America. His book had to wait for somebody to have a problem with him—because he really didn't have any of his own!

Mary Frances Shura,
*also author of **Eleanor** and*
Jefferson

● ● ●

12

THREE STEPS TO A STORY

Choosing Characters, Problems, and Solutions

As a reader, you already know that a story has a beginning, a middle, and an ending. As a writer, you need to know where to begin and how to get from one part of the story to the next.

There are many possible roads you could take. This chapter will lead you down one that many new writers find easy to follow. This isn't the only way to write a story, but it is one way, and a good one.

It requires three steps:

    1. Choose the main character;
    2. Describe the problem;
    3. Find the solution.

1. *Choose The Main Character*

A. Who—or what—could be the main character of your story? It often works best to write about the kinds of characters you like to read about. So, who—or what—are the main characters in your favorite stories?

People like yourself,
    or younger, or older?

Kings and queens,
   princes and princesses?
Creatures from outer space,
   or robots and computers?
Elves and fairies,
   giants, trolls, and ogres?
Witches, wizards,
   goblins and ghosts?
Pets, wild animals,
   farm animals, pretend animals?
Characters out of history,
   folktales, myths, and legends?
Or made-up creatures all your own?

It may not be easy to pick just one, but that's the first step. Choose a main character. Give him or her or it a name.

B. When you read a story, what do you like to know about the main character?

Here are some facts other young writers have suggested including. You may want to add to this list.

- What the character looks like.
- Where he or she lives.
- Whether the character is nice or mean.
- How old the character is.
- Whether he or she is rich, poor, or in between.
- What kind of family he or she has.
- What this character likes to do.
- Who his or her friends are.
- What this character does not like to do.

C. Begin your story by telling your readers all about

your new character. As you write, answer as many of these questions as you can, but don't worry if you can't answer them all. If your main character is a robot, for instance, it may not have any family or friends! Then again, maybe it does. It's your character, so it's all up to you.

Don't forget to include lots of details for your readers to taste, touch, smell, see, and hear. That's what makes your story come alive.

And now, your story now has a beginning.

2. Describe The Problem

A. The time has come to get your character into trouble!

Suppose he or she woke up one morning, had pleasant things happen all day, and went to bed happy that night. It would be a nice day to live, but it wouldn't make much of a story. Stories become exciting and interesting when their characters are in some kind of trouble and have to figure out a way to set things right. When the trouble comes to an end, the story does, too.

What kinds of problems might your character have?

School problems, family problems, friendship problems, health problems, money problems?

Could he or she be lost?

Lonely?
Afraid?
Trapped?
Angry?
Worried?
Sad?
Hurt?
Jealous?

Confused?

Under a spell?

Again, it's not an easy choice, but it has to be made. What one problem will your character face in this story? If you don't like any of the suggestions on the list, come up with a new one of your own.

B. As soon as you have decided on the problem, you have more decisions to make: What do you want your readers to know about the problem?

Here are some questions other writers, who, of course, are also readers, like to have answered.

- What exactly is the problem?
- How and when and where did the trouble begin?
- How long has it been going on?
- How does the main character feel about it?
- Is anyone else involved in the problem? If so, in what way? And how do these others feel about it?

C. To describe your character's problem, answer as many of these questions as you can. Add any other details you can think of to help your reader understand how things are for your character in trouble.

Your story is now well on its way.

3. *Find The Solution*

A. "If at first you don't succeed,
  try,
    try,
      again."

That's the rule for this part of your story.

If a character got into trouble at 10:00 **A.M.**, thought of a way out at 10:02, and had her life back to normal by 10:05, she might be pleased with herself, but you'd have a very short and probably dull story to tell.

If you've done a good job of getting your character into trouble, it'll take him or her more than a few minutes to get back out, and more than one or two tries. On the other hand, you don't want to keep the struggle going on so long that even your readers give up. Three tries, with the third one successful, should be just about right.

B. How do people go about trying to deal with their problems? Other young writers have suggested the following ways:

- By thinking the problem through
- By getting help from a friend, a relative, a teacher, or some kind of expert
- By fighting
- By running away
- By talking it over with whoever's causing the problem
- By changing something about themselves
- By trying to get the others involved in the problem to change
- By starting over in a new way
- By giving up
- By learning something new

C. What stands in the way of people dealing with their problems successfully? Many things. This list is just a start.

- Shortcomings inside themselves, such as
  shyness,
  fear,
  superstition,
  cowardice,
  dishonesty.

- Interference from other people, who may be
  angry,
  jealous,
  cruel,
  bossy,
  in competition,
  or who simply don't understand.

- Physical obstacles, including
  illnesses and handicaps,
    mountains that need climbing,

rivers that require crossing,
hurricanes, blizzards,
tornados, and earthquakes,
long distances to travel,
and the lack of money and time.
- Bad luck.

D. Obviously, all of these things can't happen to one character with one problem in one story. This time, though, you do get to choose THREE.

- Describe your character's first try to solve the problem. Show how and why it doesn't work. How does your character feel now?

- Describe the second try. Show how and why it doesn't work, either. And remember to include your character's feelings.

- At last, describe the third attempt. Take your time telling about this one, because this is the one that works. Your readers will want to know every little detail. And you've got brand-new feelings to report, also, the feelings of success.

You ought to know a lot about success right now, because you've just successfully written a story.

One last choice to make: your story needs a title.

13

MORE STORIES BEHIND THE STORIES

I got the idea for *Just Like a Real Family* from a picture in the Des Moines *Sunday Register*. In the photo, some lonely older men and younger boys were pictured. They'd been meeting every day in a park, and friendships had grown between the men and the boys. In *Family*, June is lonely, but her fifth grade social studies project turns out to be a foster grandparent program. June thinks it will be the answer to her loneliness. However, June is paired with grouchy old Franklin who doesn't like children. Even though I made up lots of problems, the main idea first came from the picture in the newspaper.

Kristi Holl,
*also author of **Cast a Single Shadow** and*
The Rose beyond the Wall

● ● ●

I usually say I get my ideas at the A & P. I just ask for a dozen good ideas, pay for them, and take them home.

I know where my books come from. *Chocolate Fever* began as a go-to-bed story for my daughter, Heidi. I used to tuck her into bed each night, and Heidi made me sing her silly songs. It got very boring to sing the same songs night after night. So I began to tell her five-minute, silly stories, anything not to have to sing those songs again. And one night, because Heidi and I share a passion for chocolate, I just began this story about a boy being hatched from a chocolate bean. And for the first time, I said the magic words: "to be continued."

Jelly Belly was just me getting revenge on the fat kid I used to be. I was the fattest kid in the fifth grade, and I hated it. I used some of my kids' camp experiences in it, because I never went to camp. My kids went to regular camp because they are regular size—and they hated all camps they went to.

Robert Kimmel Smith,
*also author of **The War with Grandpa***
*and **Mostly Michael***

● ● ●

I got my idea for *Ida Early* when I was writing an entirely different story and needed a chapter in which a babysitter was to look after some young children. But Ida began to more or less take over the chapter, and somehow she did not fit into the book that I was writing. Someone suggested that I leave her out of it, but that I might think about using her in a story of her own. Ten years later I got around to writing *Ida Early Comes Over the Mountain*. Perhaps ideas for the story had been accumulating in my mind during those ten years without my realizing it.

Robert Burch,
also author of **Queenie Peavy** and
D.J.'s Worst Enemy

● ● ●

Students and teachers most often ask me how I got the idea for the book, *The One And Only Autobiography of Ralph Miller, the Dog Who Knew He Was a Boy.*

The idea began quite simply from my wanting to write a story about a person who looked so different from everyone else in his community and in his family that people considered him to be no more than a dog and treated him like a dog.

It is the story of how Ralph, through determination, emerges as a person and convinces others to accept him as he really is. If the theme were written as a tragedy, it might be called *The Elephant Man.* As a drama, it might be titled *Mask.* Instead, I chose to explore the theme with humor. I think it is a very funny adventure with underlying tones of serious thought.

The book was the easiest one I've ever written. There are thirteen chapters, and I wrote one chapter a day. I'd sit down in front of the typewriter and type no more than a paragraph, then I'd begin to hear Ralph's voice as he dictated the story to me. It was wonderful fun!

David Melton,
also author and illustrator of **The One and Only**
Second Autobiography of Ralph Miller
and **Written and Illustrated by . . .**

● ● ●

73

14

A DOZEN GRAINS OF SAND

Ideas in Search of a Writer

Ideas don't come along as complete poems, plays, or stories, all ready for the writer to write them down. They come as bits and pieces—an interesting character here, an overheard conversation there, an adventure in real life or in the imagination.

An idea is a seed and remains a seed until a writer cultivates it carefully and helps it to grow. An idea is the grain of sand that gets under an oyster's shell. That same grain of sand under a lobster's shell would remain a grain of sand and nothing more. Only an oyster puts forth the extra effort required to create a pearl.

Non-writers think of it as magic: An idea falls from the sky, bounces off your head, and lands on the page, ready to read. Writers—and oysters—know better.

Here are a dozen ideas for you. Like seeds and grains of sand, they are only beginnings. It's up to you to see what you can make of them.

It's up to you to become a writer.

1. Pretend you are riding on a bus, and you suddenly overhear one person say to another, "I'll never forgive you as long as I live!"

Who are those people?

What has been said or done that is so unforgivable?

Will other people on the bus get involved in this situation?

Will you, the eavesdropper?

What happens next?

2. Imagine a tapping sound: Tap. Tap. Tap. Tap.

Where is the sound coming from?

Who is hearing it?

Does it get louder? Softer?

How does the listener feel about it?
What does he or she do about it?
And then what happens?

3. A stranger suddenly appears in the neighborhood.
Describe the stranger.
When and where is he or she first seen?
What is he or she doing?
Who is watching?
Will the neighborhood ever find out exactly who this stranger is and what he or she is up to? If so, how? If not, why not?

4. Think of a perfect place. Describe it in vivid detail.
Who is there?
What do they look like? What are they wearing?
What are they doing?
How did they get there?
How long will they stay?
If they leave, what will make them go?

5. Invent a superkid, someone who can do things no one else on earth can do. What does he or she look like?
Where does this superkid live and with whom?
What are your superkid's special powers?
Where did those powers come from?
How does your superkid use those powers? For good? For evil?
How do other people feel about Superkid?
Describe one adventure Superkid might have.

6. Imagine yourself as the winner of a contest. Your prize is five minutes on prime-time television to tell the world anything you want to say.

How do you feel?

How do you prepare for your five minutes?

What is the television studio like?

Who is there with you?

What are they all doing?

What does your five minutes on television feel like?

What do you say? How do you say it?

How do people react—those in the studio and those in your national audience?

7. Describe a meal in such delicious detail that just reading about it will make people hungry.

Include the place where it is served: a palace? a restaurant? a garden? a riverboat? a treehouse?

Show the table setting, the dishes, how the food is served, and by whom.

Who, besides your readers, is invited to dine?

8. Invent your own country.

Where is it? What does it look like? Who lives there?

Does this country have any problems? How does it deal with them?

Does it have any enemies? Who are they, and what do they want?

Consider all the aspects of running a country: water, food, shelter, trade, transportation, education, religion, health care, taxes, communication, sanitation, and so on. How does your country organize all these things?

What sort of government does it have? How does it work?

Who is in charge, and why?

9. What will you be doing in the year 2020? Describe an

entire Monday in January of that year, from the moment you wake up until the instant you fall asleep.

Does your day begin in the morning, or at night? Or can't you tell?

Where do you live?

Who is with you? Are these people you've known since the 1980's? If so, how have they changed? If not, who are these new acquaintances? And what happened to the old ones?

What do you eat?

What do you wear?

Do you work?

What changes have you seen in your lifetime, and how do you feel about them?

10. Create a character who daydreams. What does he or she daydream about, and why?

What is his or her real life like?

Do the daydreams interfere at home, at work, or at school?

Does the dreamer tell anyone about them? If so, who and why? If not, why not?

How does the dreamer feel about daydreaming?

Will he or she ever stop?

11. Imagine yourself as an astronaut assigned to spend two years at a space station. It is your job to keep a journal of your thoughts, recording what it feels like to be away from earth so long. You've been gone exactly one year today, with another year to go. What do you write in your journal for this day?

Are you remembering your life on earth? How do you feel about those memories?

How do you feel about the past year, and the year to come?

What do you do on the space station when you're not at work on your journal?

Who is there with you? Do you get along?

Begin your journal at 6:00 A.M. and make an entry for each hour until 10:00 P.M. Tell what you've done, what you've thought about, and how you feel about these things.

12. Picture a messy room, a room so messy its occupant has disappeared into the mess and cannot be found.

Describe the room, from floor to ceiling, from window to door, from wall to wall, right down to the last old sock.

Describe the room's owner. What is this person like? How and why did he or she create this mess?

Where is this person now? Will he or she ever be found? If so, how and by whom?

If not, why not? What will finally become of this messy room and its owner?

You can develop these ideas in any way you like: as poems, stories, plays, journal entries, letters to friends or fictional characters, radio or television shows—or whatever.

Feel free to change details however you wish. In #9, for instance, you might prefer to imagine yourself living in *1820*—or in 2020 *B.C.*

The point is to have fun—and to write.

You're a writer, now.

Where do you get your ideas?

15

MORE BOOKS FOR YOUNG WRITERS

A writer is rarely too young to begin or too old to improve. Learning is a lifelong process for us. There's no graduation day and no time to retire. Every minute we're awake (and some when we're asleep!) is a chance to sharpen our skills, deepen our understanding of ourselves and of life, gather ideas, dream, plan, and write. And, of course, read and read and read.

Here are some books you may find useful as you continue writing. A few are marked "out of print." You won't find them in stores anymore, but your library may have copies.

1. *Poetry*

Cosman, Anna. *How to Read and Write Poetry.* 1979. Watts. Grades 5 and up. What is poetry? What makes a good poem? This book will help you get the most out of the poems you read and write.

Hughes, Ted. *Poetry Is.* 1970. Doubleday. (Out of print.) Grades 5 and up. A poet tells how the ordinary details of life—weather, family, animals—help create poetry.

2. Plays

Judy, Susan and Stephen. *Putting on a Play, A Guide to Writing and Producing Neighborhood Drama.* 1982. Scribner. Grades 5 and up. Everything needed to put on your own show, be it a reading of favorite poems or stories or a full-length original drama.

McCaslin, Nellie. *Act Now! Plays and Ways to Make Them.* 1975. S.G. Phillips. Grades 4 and up. Easy-to-follow advice on acting, writing, and producing your own plays, skits, and stories.

3. Stories

Dubrovin, Vivian. *Write Your Own Story.* 1984. Watts. Grades 4 and up. A practical guide to story-writing technique, from "Where do I begin?" to "What do you mean, edit?"

Cheyney, Arnold. *Let's Write Short Stories.* 1973. Seamon. (Out of print.) Grades 4 and up. An easy-to-understand book highlighting the basic techniques of story writing.

Plagemann, Bentz. *How to Write a Story.* 1971. Lothrop. (Out of print.) Grades 5 and up. Nine detailed chapters on character, plot, description, conversation, and other storyteller's tools.

4. All kinds of writing

Benjamin, Carol Lea. *Writing for Kids.* 1985. Crowell (hardcover); Harper/Trophy (paperback). Grades 3 and up. Fun to read, but also filled with good advice on many aspects of writing, from keeping a notebook to creating a small book of your own.

Cassedy, Sylvia. *In Your Own Words, A Beginner's Guide to Writing.* 1979. Doubleday. Grades 6 and up. What's special about your world, and what's special about you? This book will help you find out and write about it, too.

Tchudi, Susan and Stephen. *The Young Writer's Handbook.* 1984. Scribner. Grades 7 and up. Many forms of writing are discussed—letters, fiction, plays, articles, school assignments—along with information on getting your work published.

Yates, Elizabeth. *Someday You'll Write.* 1962. Dutton. (Out of print.) Grades 4 and up. A Newbery Award winner (for *Amos Fortune, Free Man*) answers her young friends' many questions about how books are written and what it takes to be a writer.

5. *Creating your own books*

Melton, David. *Written and Illustrated by . . .* 1985. Landmark Editions. This one's for teachers, so that they can help students create books just as author Melton does in his workshops. But its many wonderful examples and illustrations from the work of young authors will make you want to get out your pencils, pens, crayons, and paintbox and get going!

Purdy, Susan. *Books for You to Make.* 1973. Lippincott. Grades 5 and up. Easily understood instructions for making your own books by hand.

6. *Others*

Aliki. *How a Book Is Made.* 1986. Crowell. Grades 2

and up. Amusing illustrations and a simple text follow a book through its various steps toward publication.

Greenfeld, Howard. *Books: From Writer to Reader.* 1976. Crown. Grades 5 and up. A fascinating look at every step in the process of publishing books.

Hanson, Mary Lewis. *Your Career as a Writer.* 1979. Arco. Grades 5 and up. Your writing skills can lead to an exciting career in journalism, advertising, radio, television, and more.

INDEX

Act Now! (McCaslin), 81
Acting out (plays), 35–36
Adler, C.S., 52, 53
Alexander, Lloyd, 11
Alone in Wolf Hollow (Brookins), 54
Anastasia Krupnik (Lowry), 13
And This Is Laura (Conford), 53
Animals, 15–18
Autumn Street (Lowry), 13

Before the Lark (Brown), 23
Beginnings (story), 64
Benjamin, Carol Lea, 81
Big Day for Rufus, A (play), 25–36
Book of Giant Stories, The
　　(Harrison), 61
Books
　by other writers, 37
　for young writers, 80–83
Books: From Writer to Reader
　　(Greenfeld), 82
Books for You to Make (Purdy), 82
Boston Public Garden, 11–12
Brains
　as idea receivers, 2–3
　ideas in, 55–60
Brookins, Dana, 54
Brown, Irene Bennett, 22–23
Burch, Robert, 72–73

Calm Horse (Cohen), 20
Calvert, Patricia, 62
Captain Morgana Mason (Francis), 38
Carly's Buck (Adler), 53
Cassedy, Sylvia, 81–82
Cast a Single Shadow (Holl), 71
Cats, 11
Character(s), 57, 58, 64–66,
　　74–75, 76
Chester (Shura), 63
Cheyney, Arnold, 81
Chocolate Fever (Smith), 71–72
Cohen, Pater Z., 20
Conford, Ellen, 53
Conversation(s), 61, 74
Cosman, Anna, 80
Curiosity, 22–23, 39

D.J.'s Worst Enemy (Burch), 73
Daydreams, 3, 58, 78
Detail(s), 57, 67, 76, 77, 79
　in characterization, 65–66
Dial Leroy Rupert, D.J. (Gilson), 22
Different ways to do things, 15–19, 50
Divine inspiration, 13
Do Bananas Chew Gum? (Gilson), 22
Dogs, 16–18
Dorothy and the Wizard of Oz, 24
Dreams, 37–38, 53
Dubrovin, Vivian, 81

Eleanor (Shura), 63
Endings (story), 64
E.T. (film), 24

Family situations, 53
Fat Glenda (Perl), 22
Fat Glenda's Summer Romance
    (Perl), 22
Feelings, 10, 13, 39, 70
Fictionalizing real situations, 38
Fingers (Sleator), 38
Flint Hills Foal, The (Francis), 38
Fourth Grade Celebrity (Giff), 38
Francis, Dorothy, 38

Giff, Patricia Reilly, 38
Gilson, Jamie, 20–22
Good-bye, Pink Pig (Adler), 52
Greenberg, Jan, 13
Greenfeld, Howard, 82

"Hotcakes for Breakfast" (poem), 6, 10
Hail, Hail, Camp Timberwood
    (Conford), 53
Handicapped persons, 23, 73
Hanson, Mary Lewis, 83
Harrison, David, 61
Hey, Remember Fat Glenda? (Perl), 22
Holl, Kristi, 71
Honestly, Myron (Hughes), 52
Hopes, 58
Horses, 20, 38
How to Read and Write Poetry
    (Cosman), 80
How to Write a Story (Plagemann), 81
Hughes, Dean, 52
Hughes, Ted, 80

I Saw Him First (Sharmat), 39
Iceberg and Its Shadow, The
    (Greenberg), 13
Ida Early Comes Over the Mountain
    (Burch), 72–73

Ideas, 5
    for animal stories, 15–18
    development of, 63, 74
    in search of a writer, 74–79
    source of, 1–3, 11
    in stories behind stories, 10–14,
        20–23, 37–39, 51–54, 61–63,
        71–73
    for writing poetry, 4–10
    in your head, 55–60
Imagination, 3, 11, 37, 40, 61, 74–79
In Your Own Words (Cassedy), 81–82
"Insulting Princess, The" (story),
    41–50
Interest (in stories), 66
Interstellar Pig (Sleator), 38
Into the Dream (Sleator), 37–38
It's a Mile from Here to Glory (Lee), 62

Jefferson (Shura), 63
Jelly Belly (Smith), 72
Journal(s), 55–60
Judy, Stephen, 81
Judy, Susan, 81
Just Another Gorgeous Guy (Brown), 23
Just Like a Real Family (Holl), 71
"Just Once More" (poem), 5

Lee, Robert C., 62
Lenny Kendall, Smart Aleck
    (Conford), 53
Let's Write Short Stories (Cheyney), 81
Libraries, 40
Life experiences, 57
Life problems, 58
Lowry, Lois, 13

McCaslin, Nellie, 81
Magic of the Glits, The (Adler), 53
Margaret's Moves (Rabe), 39
Me and Fat Glenda (Perl), 22
Melton, David, 73, 82
Memory, 3, 54
    in writing poetry, 10

Middle (story), 64
Money Creek Mare, The (Calvert), 62
Monster! Monster! (Harrison), 61
Morena (Cohen), 20
Morning Glory Afternoon (Brown), 23
Mostly Michael (Smith), 72
Muskie Hook (Cohen), 20

Nate the Great series (Sharmat), 39
News items, 61, 71
No Dragons to Slay (Greenberg), 13
Nutty for President (Hughes), 52

*One and Only Autobiography of Ralph
    Miller, The* (Melton), 73
*One and Only Second Autobiography of
    Ralph Miller, The* (Melton), 73
Outside sources of ideas, 11

Peer pressure, 13
People one knows, 22, 38, 40–41,
    56–57
"Pepper, I Said I'm Sleeping" (poem)
    8–9
Perl, Lila, 22
Personal Experience, 53, 62
Peter Pan (Barrie), 24
Pig-Out Blues, The (Greenberg), 13
Places, 76
    one has been, 57–58
Plagemann, Bentz, 81
Play writing, 24–36
    books on, 81
Poetry
    books on, 80
    how to write, 9–10
    ideas for, 4–10
Poetry Is (Hughes), 80
Problem(s) (story), 58, 64, 66–67
Prydain Chronicles, The
    (Alexander), 11
Purdy, Susan, 82
Putting on a Play (Judy and Judy), 81

Queenie Peavy (Burch), 73
Questions
    in characterization, 65–66
    for journal, 55–60
    as source of ideas, 3, 24–36, 39, 40
    in story problem, 67

Rabe, Berniece, 39
Rass (Rabe), 39
Rat Teeth (Giff), 38
Reading, 3, 62, 64–65
Real-life situations, 52
Research, 40
Revision, 10, 36
Rhyme, 10, 50
Rico's Cat (Brookins), 54
Rose beyond the Wall, The (Holl), 71
Run from a Scarecrow (Brown), 22

Schools, 13, 20–22, 38, 62
Science fiction, 37
Senses, 57, 66
Setting(s), 58
Sharmat, Marjorie Weinman, 39
Shura, Mary Frances, 63
Sight, 10, 57, 66
Sleator, William, 37–38
"Sly as a Pox" (poem), 7–8
Smells, 10, 57, 66
Smith, Robert Kimmel, 71–72
Snowbird, The (Calvert), 62
Solutions, 64, 67–70
Someday You'll Write (Yates), 82
*Son of the Slime Who Ate Cleveland,
    The* (Sharmat), 39
Sounds, 10, 57, 66, 75–76
Split Sisters (Adler), 53
Stone Pony, The (Calvert), 62
Stories behind stories, 11–14, 20–23,
    37–39, 51–54, 61–63, 71–73
Story writing
    books in, 81
    steps in, 64–70

Summer of the Green Star, The
(Lee), 62
"Surprise" (poem), 6–7
Switching Tracks (Hughes), 52

Taking Care of Terrific (Lowry), 13
Tape-recording, 36
Taste, 10, 57, 66
Tchudi, Stephen, 82
Tchudi, Susan, 82
Thirteen Ways to Sink a Sub
(Gilson), 22
Thoughts, 10
Time Cat (Alexander), 11
Timequake (Lee), 62
Title(s), 10, 70
To All My Fans, with Love, from Silvie
(Conford), 53
Touch, 57, 66
Travel, 3, 57–58

Wake Up, Sun! (Harrison), 61
War with Grandpa, The
(Smith), 72
Warning, The (Francis), 38
Ways to do things, 3, 4–10

Weinman, Nathan "Nate", 39
Westmark (Alexander), 11
"What would happen if" ideas, 3,
24–36, 50, 58
"*Who Killed Sack Annie?*
(Brookins), 54
"Why" ideas, 3, 40–50, 58–59
Why Me? (Conford), 53
Wild Night (Cohen), 20
Winter Worm Business, The (Giff), 38
Wishes, 58
Write Your Own Story (Dubrovin), 81
Writers
idea sources of, 1–3
Writers, young
books for, 80–83
Writing for Kids (Benjamin), 81
Writing Poetry, 9–10
Writing to discover, 40–50
Written and Illustrated by . . . (Melton),
73, 82

Yates, Elizabeth, 82
Young Writer's Handbook (Tchudi and
Tchudi), 82
Your Career as a Writer (Hanson), 83

ABOUT THE AUTHOR

Sandy Asher is a novelist, a playwright, and a poet. She is also the mother of Benjamin and Emily. She teaches and lectures at schools, conferences, and colleges, and her husband, Harvey, is a professor.

Born in Philadelphia, the author received her B.A. from Indiana University and did graduate study at the University of Connecticut. Now she lives and teaches in Springfield, Missouri, where she is writer-in-residence at Drury College.

Asher's plays have been published and produced on diverse stages from universities to arts festivals. Her seven novels for young readers have appeared in both hardback and paperback editions. Her writing has won many recognitions and awards.

Says Sandy Asher, "I credit my teachers . . . with instilling in me the confidence needed to write. I write for young people, because I know the characters in books are often the only trustworthy friends they have."